VA

GOAL SETTING

How to DREAM BIG and
Live the Life You Were
Meant to Live

5 Steps to
Discovering Your Core Values and
Living Your BEST LIFE EVER

By

Stephanie Dee Smith

Values Based Goal Setting
How to DREAM Big and Live the Life You Were Meant to Live
5 Steps to Discovering Your Core Values and Living Your BEST LIFE EVER

For more information and resources,
visit www.valuesbasedgoalsettingbook.com and www.thepinkbriefcase.com
or reach out to stephaniedee@thepinkbriefcase.com

Printed in the United States of America
First Printing 2020
First Edition 2020

ISBN 978-0-578-73266-4

For Jim, who has always believed in me

Table of Contents

PREFACE

Before We Get Started

I have worked in government for over 30 years, so trust me when I say this. Government can be the place where your dreams go to die. It doesn't have to be, but it can. Why? Because government is a large organization. Large organizations have rules. Large organizations have laws they have to follow. Large organizations have policies. Large organizations have p-r-o-c-e-d-u-r-e-s! Large organizations have a million little nuances that can, after a time, grow wearisome.

Do any of you work in large organizations? Are any of you struggling to find your place amidst a sea of regulations? Do any of you feel as there is something bigger out there that you just can't quite put your finger on? Are any of you weary?

If so, please keep reading. I wrote this book for you.

Not that I am weary. Absolutely not. In fact, I am anything but weary. I am excited! I am invigorated! I get up in the morning thinking "I actually get PAID to have this much fun at work."

How is that possible, you say?

I mean let's be real here. Most people do not have that much enthusiasm for their jobs after the first month, let alone almost 35 years. You're thinking I can't possibly be serious.

But I am.

I love what I do.

And just exactly what is that, you ask? What is the secret government job that leaves its employees feeling euphoric, at least 99% of the time?

Are you ready?

Wait for it....

This is important so pay attention....

I SERVE.

That's right. I serve others.

It's as simple as that.

What I do, no matter the task, is in service to someone else.

Oh sure, part of why I go to work every day is because like most people, I enjoy having a roof over my head and food in the refrigerator. But that's only part of it. I can work anywhere. I was looking for a job when I found this one. I believe in my skills. I believe in my ability to always find work when I need it.

The thing is, I enjoy what I do because I enjoy serving others. No matter what job I have, if I can find the service component of it, I will enjoy myself. I will be happy. I will feel fulfilled.

You might say, I VALUE serving others. It is important to me. It is something that gets me really excited about life.

And that my friends, is what life is all about.

Finding that one thing, or two things, or ten things, that get you really excited about life and doing more of them.

It isn't about money. In fact, they say a wealthy person who isn't happy is poor indeed. And a poor person who is profoundly grateful is wealthy beyond measure.

Finding the things you value, the things you would give almost anything to have more of, is the key to finding happiness. To paraphrase Confucius (or Mark Twain depending on what source you cite) it is the key to never having to work another day in your life.

Don't get lost in the weariness of life. Take this journey with me to find out what you value. Let's discover together what truly has the power to make you happy.

SECTION 1

Chapter 1

In the beginning....

"The most difficult thing is the decision to act., the rest is merely tenacity."

~ Amelia Earhart ~

Every one of us was created for some great purpose. Whether you find the source of your inspiration in God, or Spirit, or the Universe, or your friends, or your family, there is something BIG in all of us. At some point in our lives we have all felt that silent nudge. It starts like a quiet pull on our soul – a constant, almost sub-conscious reminder that tells us we should be doing something more with our lives.

The longer we ignore it, the louder it gets.

Eventually, it becomes this screaming banshee that won't let us sleep at night.

These are our big dreams!

If you are like me, you have listened to this big dream. You have said to yourself, "I want to be an artist."

"I want to move to Montana and buy a cattle ranch."

"I want to be a doctor."

"I want...."

You may have even said it out loud.

Maybe you shared your big dream with those around you.

Some of you might have taken the brazen step of writing it down, setting it as an intention, or making it a SMART Goal (We'll talk more about SMART Goals and why they're not helping later).

You definitely put it on the top of your New Year's Resolution a few years ago.

And the next year.

And the next year.

And the next.

But… the big dream doesn't materialize.

What gives?

Well, life gets in the way.

You think of a million reasons why you can't make it happen.

Maybe you are not cut out to be an artist.

You don't know a thing about cattle ranching.

Medical school is way too expensive.

You are not creative enough to bring the big dream to life.

Well friends, that is where you are wrong. And if you wait long enough, you are going to be DEAD WRONG.

Life is a creative process. We are all creative beings. And that doesn't have to mean art or music or literature.

The very act of starting a business is creative. Designing a better automobile is creative. Building a healthy body is creative.

Why?

Because we are all simply made of cells and tissues. And if I remember my high school biology correctly, cells and tissues are formed, live, and die, every day.

Every single day is an opportunity to use those new cells in an exciting way. Every single day is an opportunity to rebuild what has been torn down in your mind.

Every single day is a chance to create something new with your life. Every single day is a chance to resurrect those big dreams and begin creating the life you were meant to live.

You're past that, you say?

You tried it once and it failed?

I have news for you, my friends. There is no rule that says you missed your opportunity so boy oh boy, too bad.

Your one big chance came up in 2008 and you missed it, so you are out of luck and you can't move forward now.

Nope. Not true.

If it were true, why are you still thinking about your big dream? If it were true, why do you still hear that nagging, quiet voice in your soul? If it were true, why are you still setting the same goals over and over again?

Somewhere deep inside, you KNOW that you were meant for more.

You KNOW that there is something you were created to do.

You KNOW that you won't be able to get it out of your head until you accomplish whatever it is you have dreamed about.

It is time you listened.

It is time you acted.

It is time for you to live the life you were meant to live.

It is time to stop goal setting and start goal getting, don't you think?

The time is always right to do the right thing.

Don't you think your big dream is definitely the right thing?

After all, if you do follow your dreams, no matter how long you have been ignoring them, you will find yourself in prestigious company. Lots of people changed direction, at all stages of their lives. Did you know that Walt Disney was a newspaper editor before he realized his dream of building an amusement park?

Julia Child was a CIA Intelligence Operator, i.e., A SPY, before she taught us all how to debone a duck.

Ellen DeGeneres was a paralegal.

Andrea Bocelli and John Grisham were lawyers.

Whoopi Goldberg was a funeral home makeup artist.

And Sylvester Stallone cleaned out the lion cages at the Central Park Zoo before writing and starring in his epic character role, Rocky Balboa. Talk about following your dreams!

When we think about it, we are all just trying to make a difference, while still being able to pay our mortgages. Some of us want to buy cool cars, take wild trips around the globe, or do whatever else gets us super stoked about life. Some of us want to get married, have children, or not, raise children, or not, put children through college etc.

Amidst all that we set goals. We try and accomplish things that we think will get us closer to our goals. We read books, we set our vision boards, act SMART, etc.

So, how is that working for you? How is SMART working?

Let's talk about that.

Chapter 2

The Value of Goals

"If you want to be happy, set a goal that commands your thoughts, liberates your energy, and inspires your hopes"

~ Andrew Carnegie ~

Before we get into the details about SMART goal setting, and why SMART just does not work, lets first look at the value of goals in general. Because goals DO matter. That is the whole point of this book, after all.

If your goals aren't working for you, keep reading. Because I think you'll see it's not the goal that's causing the problem, but the way you see the goal that's keeping you from living the life you were meant to live.

Goals matter because....

***Goals create the road map to our life*.**

If we know where we are going, it easier to get there. By stating what it is we want, we can channel our energies in the right direction. For example, say you wanted to run a marathon. With that as the goal, you would at least know you needed some basic running background. You would know you probably shouldn't eat that third cupcake at the office birthday party the day before your long run.

Knowing the goal, you have a general idea of what you should be doing to get there.

In a way, having goals is like changing the lens on your life's camera. Most of the time we use the standard lens that comes with the camera. I am talking DSLR cameras now, not the one that comes with your phone, although I know they have zoom lenses for those now too.

Anyway, back to the lens. We use what comes in the box. It works okay. It takes the picture. But it doesn't capture everything. It doesn't zoom in to the really good stuff. Having a goal takes you out of the standard lens of life, puts on the zoom, and focuses on the good stuff.

Goals help us budget our resources.

It is hard to do everything. It is certainly hard to do everything at the same time. It seems there is never enough time, never enough money, never enough of *something* you need to get the job done. Knowing the goal provides the guidance you need to spend your time and money wisely.

For example, let's go back to the marathon. I am sure there are some aspiring marathoners out there. I was once one myself. For a minute. The office cupcakes got to me. But that is another story.

If I *were* to run a marathon, though, I would need new and better shoes. And a running coach. And lifetime access to my chiropractor. Knowing my goal was to run a marathon helps me budget my extra dollars to fund the shoes. I wouldn't buy a new set of high heels for the office before I bought a new pair of running shoes. I also wouldn't hire a running coach before I had a good pair of running shoes. Understanding the goal helps prioritize our limited resources.

The end result? Allocating our resources wisely helps us achieve our goals faster.

Goals can slow the clock.

Time is our most precious resource. How we spend that time has a direct correlation on how successful we are in achieving our big dreams. As Henry David Thoreau, the American essayist and poet once said, "It's not enough to be busy. So are the ants. The question is: what are we busy about."

Goals help you budget your time - just like money, just like any other resource. Keeping a clear picture of your goal can actually create more time to work on it by forcing out any activities that are not helping you cross the finish line.

Goals provide the measuring stick.

Say your goal is to run that marathon by the time you are 30. Your 30th birthday is a date fixed in time. That is an obvious measuring stick for whether you meet the goal or not. But it doesn't have to be such a dramatic goal, or a dramatic measuring stick, to be effective. Say you are an entrepreneur and your goal is to build your social media following. Having a specific number in mind, plus assigning a date to when you hope to accomplish this can be the jumpstart you need to get it done.

Finally, goals improve communication.

Being honest about your goals helps those around know what you are up to. It also helps you stay committed when you make your goals public. If I had shared my once, brief goal of running a marathon with *anyone*, I would be forever living it down because I was definitely not committed to that goal. Perhaps if I had, I would have been more inclined to train, get the professional coaching I needed, etc.

Truthfully, I did not share my brief flirtation with running a marathon with anyone because I really didn't want to run a marathon. I only thought I wanted to run a marathon. But if running a marathon had been a real, values-based goal for me, at that moment in my life, telling people would have been the first step in getting help when I needed it. We are going to cover this in depth in Step 4, but if you truly care about your goal, tell people. Write it down, share with those around you, and make sure you let people know that you need their support.

But as we will see later, even making your goals public does not guarantee their accomplishment. If the goal isn't the right goal, or you aren't viewing it through the right lens, every drop of energy, every penny of investment you spend on it, will be for nothing. Because you will not get there. I will even be so bold as to claim you CAN'T get there.

Goals Matter

I am not telling you any of this to hurt your feelings or imply that you have been wasting your time on purpose, or heaven forbid, are lazy. I'm telling you this because without a real understanding of what motivates you, what drives you to take certain actions, what you value, AT YOUR CORE, you will never be able to move past the dream into the reality of living your best life.

Let's get real. Goals are important. Without them, we would all just be giant couch potatoes.

But if goal setting were so valuable to us, or so easy to do, wouldn't we be achieving more of them?

Maybe, just maybe, we should re-think the WAY we go about setting our goals.

Enter the age of SMART

We have all seen them before. Anyone who has taken any kind of goal-setting workshop or read a goal-setting book written in the last few decades knows that SMART Goals are: Specific, Measurable, Actionable, Realistic, and Time-Related.

But where did SMART come from?

SMART first appeared in an article entitled: "There's a S.M.A.R.T. Way to Write Management's Goals and Objectives" in 1981. George T. Doran, the "father" of SMART Goals, was a former Director of Corporate Planning for the Washington Water and Power Company. He explained that the best way to achieve your goals was to break them down into small steps that each could be measured against the SMART model.

In theory it makes sense. Break your goal down into manageable steps and then assign a measurable time frame to each component. The problem is that SMART was created to improve production at a factory.

A *factory!* And not just any factory, but a *GOVERNMENT FACTORY!* Processing widgets or some such thing. Hardly the stuff that big dreams are made of. Remember what I told you about working in government? Government is often the place where big dreams go to die. It should be no surprise that I have set a lot of SMART goals over the past 30 years.

Why?

Because there are a lot of time management experts tell us that if we do these things, when we set our goals, we will achieve them. We will be focused, we will be centered, we will have a road map for success.

But do we? Has SMART really been our road map for success? We only have to look back to the New Year's resolutions to see that maybe the experts are wrong.

I am going to repeat what I said, "In the Beginning", because it is important:

"Maybe you shared your big dream with those around you.

Some of you might have taken the brazen step of writing it down, setting it as an intention, or making it a SMART Goal.

You definitely put it on the top of your New Year's Resolution a few years ago.

And the next year.

And the next year.

And the next.

But... the big dream doesn't materialize. Life gets in the way. You think of a million reasons why you can't make it happen.

Maybe you are not cut out to be an artist.

You don't know a thing about cattle ranching.

Medical school is way too expensive.

You are not creative enough to bring the big dream to life.

Well friends, that is where you are wrong. And if you wait long enough, you are going to be DEAD WRONG."

SMART came out in 1981. Essentially, we have been blowing our goals for almost 40 years.

Chapter 3

Beyond SMART – Why traditional goal setting isn't working

"Setting Goals is the first step in turning the invisible into the visible."

~ Tony Robbins ~

SMART Goals were designed for optimizing business performance. SMART Goals are science-based. SMART Goals only look at the outcomes. SMART Goals are inflexible. SMART Goals only work if your goal is leading you in the right direction.

In a nutshell, SMART Goals are boring. No offense to Mr. Doran.

So, if SMART Goals only work if your goal is leading you in the right direction, what is the wrong direction?

The wrong direction is anything that takes you away from your big dream. The wrong direction is anything that feels forced or anxiety ridden. The wrong direction is anything that is opposite of where you feel most comfortable and true to yourself. It is opposite of where you are authentic. The wrong direction is anywhere that does not honor, fulfill, and reinforce your **core values**.

Please do not misunderstand. I am not implying that all your previous goals were bad. Goals that conflict with your core values may be noble. They may be in the best interest of someone you care about. They may even be something you *want to do*. After all, I wanted to run a marathon. Well, thought I wanted to anyway.

Anyway, my point is, however noble or righteous or freakin' awesome your goals may be, if they conflict with your core values, you are never going to get there.

Because your values are going to stop you.

Your core values are going to send you in the opposite direction.

Every. Single. Time.

How do they do this?

Excuses Dressed Like Logic and Reason

Let me explain.

When I wanted to run a marathon, I laid out a training plan. There are literally dozens, probably hundreds, maybe even thousands of them online you can download, some of them for free. Obviously I wasn't going to start with a marathon. I was going to start with getting off the couch. Seriously. I downloaded an app called Couch to 5K. If your goal is to run a 5K, I highly recommended it.

Every day I walked/ran the requisite number of miles until I was actually able to run 3 miles in a single session. For those of you metrically challenged like I am, a 5K is 3.1 miles. It was awesome. Phase 1 – CHECK!

But then I had to move from a 5K to a 10K. Whoops.

Enter the excuses.

"It's really wet outside today. You don't want to get sick. Plus, your back is still a little sore after you took that tumble last week. You should give it more time to rest."

Yeah. That's right. I should rest.

"You know, there is a great new restaurant opening in town tomorrow. You should go with your friends and check it out."

Yeah. That's right. I've been so busy doing this 5K thing I have been neglecting my friends.

And there it is. I just signed the death certificate for my marathon.

But here is the thing. If running a marathon was something that honored my core values, I would have moved heaven and earth to get out there and train. The 5K wasn't even that hard, really. When I look back on it, it only took about six weeks to go from the couch to running 3.1 miles three times a week. That is pretty awesome.

But one of my core values is **family.** More specifically, *time* with my family. Every 3-mile run took an hour out of my day when you factor in changing, warming up, cooling down, and showering. This was in addition to the 3 ½ hours a day I spent commuting at the time on some of Southern California's worst freeways. As healthy as running nearly 10 miles a week was for my body, it wasn't something that honored my core value of time with my family. I had to squeeze it in. I looked for ways to do it when my husband wasn't home. I had a goal to run a marathon. But I hadn't tied the goal to a core value. Frankly, I hadn't tied it to anything, other than something I thought of one day, and thought, "cool, I wanna try that."

Subconsciously, I knew that I would never run a marathon. Consciously, I used logic and reason to kill that goal. No one could fault me for it. It made perfect sense. Some of my family probably even thought, "what was she thinking" when they saw me running a Couch to 5K. And that is okay. Because it was not a values-based goal.

But what if it had been?

Well, you would probably be reading a book right now about how to run a marathon.

Chapter 4

What are Core Values and How do they Influence our Goals?

"It does not do to leave a live dragon out of your calculations, if you live near one."

~ J.R.R. Tolkien ~

When I was younger, I owned a landscape maintenance business. I was between government jobs, it was during an economic downturn, and I couldn't find work in my field. My husband had started this business a few years earlier on his days off because he wanted a new car and I told him we couldn't afford it. He went out and got 6 people to pay him $50 bucks a month to mow their lawns, and voila, Mr. Smith's Lawn & Landscape was born.

I started helping him on Fridays, and we started getting more customers. Eventually, we had enough customers that I was working by myself the other days of the week, sometimes with a girlfriend who wanted to earn some extra cash, and at the height of our business we were mowing up to 40 lawns per week.

Let me tell you, there are plenty of lessons in the garden. In fact, one of my valuable life philosophies was revealed to me while mowing someone else's lawn almost 20 years ago.

Never Fight a Goat Over a Patch of Grass

One of our customers owned an agricultural piece of land that had a HUGE backyard. In the far reaches of the yard was a goat tethered to a pole. The problem was, his tether was just long enough that when I got to that portion of the lawn, he could reach me. Being the city girl that I was raised to be, I went up to the goat and said hi. The goat was indifferent. Until I turned my back of course and pushed the lawn mower away from him. Then he reared up and head butted me in the rear end. I fell to the ground but was more startled than anything. When I got up and finished that stretch of lawn and turned around to come back, you know that little dickens did it again!

You see, to me, that patch of grass was just a task that had to be checked off. To the goat, that patch of grass was his dinner! In short, that patch of grass meant more to him that it would ever mean to me. I was interested in the grass. He was INVESTED. For him it had significant value. For me, meh.

What is a Value?

Merriam-Webster has two definitions of the word "value" that are important to the goal setting exercise.

1. relative worth, utility, or importance

2. something (such as a principle or quality) intrinsically valuable or desirable

The word intrinsic is key here. Intrinsic means it is natural. It is inborn. It is part of who you are. It is a DNA-coded part of your being. Another word for intrinsic in inherent. Things that are inherent are even more important to who you are and what you want from life because the word inherent has a legal definition. Under the law, things that are inherent are vested in you as a right or privilege.

So identifying your intrinsic, inherent, core values is critical to understanding you as a person, and helping you focus your energies on goals that stand any chance of success. You have both a God-given, and legal right to live your best life. Don't you think it's time to start exercising that right?

In other words, what is *your* patch of grass?

There are literally thousands of principles or qualities sometimes referred to as values and none of them are more important than the other. What gives them importance is the *value* the individual places on them.

To simplify, I have broken these principles (values) down into four categories:

Virtuous values include things such as justice, equality, gratitude, love, forgiveness, mercy, freedom, sympathy, charity, faith, patience, humility, and kindness.

Philosophical values speak to your outlook toward life. Beliefs such as hard work, diligence, self-reliance, commitment, determination, security, allegiance, loyalty, tenacity, and courage are all philosophical values.

Social values reflect how you interact with others, particularly those you work with or are in relationship with. Examples of social values include teamwork, respect, competition, leadership, equity, liberality, friendship, abundance, and communication.

Aesthetic values describe your appreciation of the world around you and how you approach life. Things such as beauty, creativity, fun, pleasure, satisfaction, prosperity, innovation, artistry, and resourcefulness are all aesthetic values.

All of these could be core values to an individual. But they are not all core to everyone. I will explain why in a minute.

Values provide the ultimate sense of purpose for our lives. Bring to mind anything or anyone that is important to you, your patch of grass if you will. Whoever that person or whatever that thing is, can be tied directly to one of these (or similar) values.

Our values keep us on track. Our values keep us from making decisions that will cost us, emotionally, financially, spiritually. Our values, when honored, make us happy, whole, and authentic.

I mentioned earlier that I value my family and fiercely protect the time I spend with them. To me *family* is a virtuous value. Because ultimately, family is about love. True, unadulterated, forgiving, merciful love. For others, family might not rank high at all, because they lived a different life than I lived. They have different experiences. There are no right or wrong values, and values that are core to one person might not even make the top 50 for another. You are likely starting to see that values are deeply personal.

How Are Values Formed?

Earlier I said that core values are intrinsic, or inherent. That they are natural, almost inbred, and DNA-coded into our being. We are born with them. Don't we all know that one child that has been kind and compassionate and gentle their whole life? What about the assertive, leadership driven teen that has been "bossy" since they were a toddler? I am sure you can think of other examples of values, disguised as behaviors, that bear witness in our own lives.

But our values can also come from the way we were raised. While it is true that most core values are intrinsic, many of our most important values, ones that we will often identify as core, are actually inherited values. Inherited values are things like religion, faith, family, education, money. Just like blue eyes and red hair, some inherited characteristics are as natural to our being as can be. They cannot be changed, no matter how hard we try.

Let me give you an example. Keith is a friend of mine. He was raised by a single mom who worked two jobs just to keep him and his brothers in food and clothes. Because of how he was raised, he grew up with a deep sense of fear around spending money. Even though he was highly successful as an emergency room nurse, and earned close to six figures before overtime, he was always concerned he would never have enough. As a result, he lived like a pauper. He rented a room in a buddy's house, bought his clothes at the thrift store, drove a beater car, and never, repeat never, took a vacation. For Keith, financial security was an inherited value, but one he definitely considered core.

Enter Julie, another nurse at the same hospital. Julie adored Keith and at first thought his quirkiness about money was "cute". She also had been raised in a poor family and had worked two jobs just to pay for nursing school. Unlike Keith, though, who was constantly worrying about money, Julie had this deep sense of peace knowing there would always be enough. She enjoyed fun, and a free-wheeling lifestyle. After I met her for the first time, I could tell that she held pleasure and enjoying life on her terms as core values. Knowing her background, you would never say she learned those things from the way she was raised. She had always felt that way, and even though things on the surface sometimes looked bleak, her sense of joy and peace radiated from her core, and she was happy. Her sense of peace and joie de vivre was intrinsic.

But here is the thing. Keith was happy too, living the way he did. Remember, there are no right or wrong values. What is important to one person does not have to be important to the next. What makes one person immensely happy could drive their friends or even other family members absolutely bonkers.

By now you can see where this story is going though, right? As much as Keith liked Julie, and much as Julie adored Keith, he just could not deal with her spendthrift behaviors. He found himself judging her for buying a new purse when the five she already had were fine. She thought his quirkiness was cute, but really wished he would get his own place, so they had more privacy.

They argued over little things, but deep down it always boiled down to their approach over money.

Their values clashed. Big time. And so their great love story was finished before it ever had a chance to really get started.

Is there something in your life that you're just not happy with? It doesn't have to be a romance. Maybe it's your job. Or where you live. Or your health. Understanding your values, and those you hold at your deepest core, is critical to finding true happiness in your life. Understanding your core values, and using them to set values-based goals, are key to living the life you not only want to live, but were *meant* to live.

The Internal Struggle

Maybe you have done some values identification work before, and you think you know what your core values are, but you are still not reaching your goals. It could be that you're facing the internal struggle between different kinds of values.

Inherited values are important, but on the surface even they can conflict with our intrinsic values. Think of it as nature versus nurture values. There are different kinds of values, and when they compete against each other, intrinsic values will always win.

Imagine if Keith had been the one born with an intrinsic value of pleasure-seeking and fun no matter what? He would constantly be battling his desire for fun with his need for financial security. And guess which one would "win"? Yes, that's right. The intrinsic one. He would go out and spend money, perhaps buy things he didn't need, live life to the fullest, but he wouldn't enjoy it. Why? Because he would feel guilty when his inherited core values of financial security and thrift reared their head and strongly suggested to him that he was making a mistake.

Don't worry about Keith though. He eventually met someone just like him. Susie loves living the simple life, and she was raised as an outdoors girl. She convinced Keith to invest some of his nest egg in some vacant land in the country, but close to the highway, and they built a beautiful, two story, completely off-grid log home. They own it cash out right and Keith is happy that he is even saving money over his previous rented room situation.

Julie met a firefighter in the emergency room and this man has absolutely no problem spending money. They get along great, and even though some might look at them and think they are on shaky financial ground, living paycheck to paycheck, they are at least enjoying themselves.

Values are personal and individual. They are simply *principles* that a person *assigns a value* to, based on their individual experiences and make-up. Values are not right or wrong. It is what we do with those values that can be perceived by others as right or wrong. Once you know what your true, core values are, however, you will find you don't really care what others think. You will know that your true happiness lies in being true to your values and living the life you were created to live.

The Relationship Between Goals and Values.

Goals change all the time, right? What about our values?

Typically, no. Our values do not change. But we can change which values we prioritize based on where we are in our life at any given moment.

Let's start with an easy one. Let's say you value money, like my friend Keith. We don't need to go into why you value money because values aren't right or wrong. Maybe like Keith you grew up in extreme poverty and see money as a means of security, for things as basic as food and shelter. The "why" is important to you, but it isn't important to us.

So, you value money. Your goals are going to be dependent upon where you are in your life right now. If you don't have enough money for basic needs, you are going to set goals around increasing the amount of money you have. Things like find a better paying job, start a side business, reduce expenses.

If you have enough money for the basics, your goals are going to be focused on having more money for the other things you value. Because here is the thing. No one values money for the money. After all, it is just paper, or a tiny bit of metal. They value money for the things it can buy them. Things like food, shelter, clothing. Things like vacations, recreation, or college for their kids. Maybe they like a new car every four years. Yeah, that is a thing. Who knew?

At the end of the day, people value money because it funds their dreams. They can buy expensive wine or live in a particular community or retire from their jobs and babysit their grandchildren. They value money for the experiences it can provide. Their goals are going to reflect those dreams, those experiences they long for.

Let's look at another example. In addition to valuing time with my family, I also hold justice as a core value. One way to live in honor of my value for justice would be to go into law. That means going to law school. That means at least three years of intense study. That means spending over $100,000 for a degree that based on my age, I would likely use for around 10-15 years after I graduated. Yeah. That's just not going to happen.

Not that it couldn't. It absolutely could. I could set a goal around becoming an attorney and go to law school and incur the debt and pass the bar exam and voila! I've reached my goal. But the goal itself is flawed. The goal itself violates too many other core values. (Family, prosperity, freedom).

Does that mean I give up on my core value of justice? Absolutely not. I find lots of ways to honor that value. I volunteer with a group that helps facilitate visits between children and their incarcerated parents. I answer the call when summoned for jury duty. I vote responsibly for elected leaders and legislation that honor my commitment to justice.

There are lots of ways that we can honor our core values, without setting goals that are obvious, what would be expected, or what other people are doing.

What kinds of dreams (goals) are you holding in your heart?

Goals are flexible. Values are not.

I mentioned this earlier, but this is another point I am going to repeat because it too is important. Your goals are dependent on what you value, and where you are in life.

Wait, let me clarify.

Achievable goals depend on what you value, and where you are in life. Let's be real. I could set a goal to be an astronaut. I value innovation, and I am at a point in my life where I want to seriously contribute to improving the world around me. But....that goal isn't achievable because 1 – my college degree is not in STEM (science, technology, engineering or math); and 2 – there is no way in hell you would get me to sit on top of a pile of explosives in a metal can manufactured by the lowest bidder. No way. But God bless the ones who do, because I think space exploration is cool!

Individual personalities, and timing, are everything. That is why goals change, and values stay constant!

If goals are like our road map, values are our compass. They tell us where true north is. They point us in the right direction. Creating goals that honor and amplify your values make them more attainable. And isn't that what everyone wants? To reach their goals?

If so, it's time to stop goal setting and start goal getting. But we can't do that without looking at our values and deciding which ones we want to prioritize at this point in our lives.

Did I mention there are thousands, if not tens of thousands, of values words? Knowing which values are important to you is critical to setting goals that are beyond SMART. Meaning 1) not boring; and 2) truly fulfilling.

Chapter 5

Why We Need to Dream Big

"If you can dream it, you can do it!"

~ Walt Disney ~

We have already talked about why SMART goals are boring. Let's face it, your best life isn't going to be defined by how many iPhones you sold at the Apple store you worked at when you were 25. Your best life isn't defined by whether you lost that 20 pounds you gained at Christmas before Valentine's Day. But, your best life IS going to be defined by the experiences you had, the people you shared them with, the smiles you brought to other people's faces, and the inspiration you provided to strangers that you may never meet.

Setting goals that align with your best life requires that you set aside any preconceived limitations. Now is the time to DREAM BIG. Stop making excuses for why your dreams can't come true. And if you do make excuses, stop using logic and reason to justify them. Dreams are not logical. Big dreams are not reasonable.

Stop worrying about what people are going to think. The only person whose opinion matters in this exercise is YOURS. YOU are the dreamer! You are the person that you have to answer to. You are the pilot of your life's journey. You are the captain of your own ship.

I know what you are thinking. You're thinking "well I have a spouse I have to think about" Or "I have children I have to provide for" or even "Dreams are great but how am I going to pay the bills?"

I am going to get a little in your face right now and tell you, none of that is going to matter if you spend your entire life trying to meet other people's expectations of you.

Why?

Because when we are not doing the things we love, not having the experiences we crave, not living the life we were meant to have, or living up to the dreams that are already inside of us, we are never going to enjoy living.

And if we don't enjoy living, we sometimes aren't particularly good at it.

We don't perform well at work.

Our relationships are crap.

We drive those we care about out of our lives.

Our entire universe suffers because we won't honor the purpose that I believe lives in each of us.

You read about it all the time. Adult children who came from dysfunctional or abusive homes perpetuate the cycle. All because one parent thought it was better to "stay together for the kids" rather than leave and start a happier life for everyone.

Or people who actually make themselves physically ill because they are so unhappy. High blood pressure, heart disease, obesity, diabetes, etc. are all on the rise because people are stressed out and don't know how to handle life.

Is that your big dream?

Of course not.

You were made for so much more.

How do I know this? Because you are here, drawing breath, reading this book.

You are still on the right side of the grass.

You don't even have to be a religious person to ask yourself, "if you had accomplished everything you were created to accomplish, would you still be here?"

Whether you have one day or fifty years left in this life, don't you want to spend it doing things that honor your values and feed your soul?

Now is the time to dream big. Small goals are great, and they help move us along in life, but they rarely achieve that life-altering purpose that we are all carrying around inside. So no dreaming things like a new outfit, or a puppy, or a new office. That is unless that new office comes with a big fat promotion or owning your own company.

To start living the life you were meant to live you must give power to the dreams you have been carrying deep in your soul your entire life. The quiet, hidden meditations of your heart. The things that only you and your Creator know about.

Those are the dreams I am talking about.

Game changer

Dreaming big dreams and believing you can achieve them is life changing. Setting values-based goals is the first step in living a values-based life. Living a values-based life is the key to looking back at the end and saying, "good job". And, perhaps more importantly, it is the key to being happy along the way.

I am not telling you anything you don't already know. You're reading this book because you know that traditional goal setting isn't working for you. You know you have something big inside you want to accomplish and you just haven't been able to move forward. You know this because you are still setting the same New Year's Resolution every single year.

I know I was.

I can look back over decades of notebooks and journals where I would capture my hopes and dreams. I had set goals like write a book, lose 80 pounds, be a City Manager, etc. And none of them materialized. Oh, I might lose 20 pounds on whatever fad diet was making the rounds that year. Or I might make a list of books I would like to write. Or I might peruse a job announcement that came across my desk at City Hall (not in the Manager's office). But I wasn't making any significant progress. I always gave up. Sometimes by Super Bowl Sunday. Always by the time Easter rolled around.

Why? Because I wasn't tying the goal to my values.

It was only when I realized my values were what were holding me back that things started to change. And, then it hit me. Like a ton of bricks. If my values were keeping me from achieving my goals, my values could also help point the way to goals that mattered. Or if my goals were already good, my values could help frame them in such a way that they suddenly became achievable.

My values put purpose into my life.

So how do you find that purpose?

You start by dreaming big dreams.

You start by listening to that still small voice in your soul that says, "you can do THIS!"

You start by asking yourself "what would I do if I knew I could not fail."

SECTION 2

Chapter 6

Step 1 – Spend Some Time with Yourself

"The only light in this dark night is that which burns in the soul. And that is a guide more certain than the mid-day sun."

~ St. John of the Cross, Dark Night of the Soul ~

The first step in discovering your core values is to spend some time alone with yourself. No one else can tell you what your values are. No one else can define your patch of grass.

Values cannot be top down, like from a boss or supervisor. Or from a partner, or family member. They have to be bottom up, or inside out, coming directly from you to the outside world.

Why? Because the outside rarely changes the inside, but the inside ALWAYS affects the outside. Think of decaying fruit. Usually the decay starts on the inside and you don't even know the apple has gone bad until you bite in through its still firm outer skin. In our own bodies when we're sick, the damage usually starts deep inside long before it shows up in outward symptoms.

Trying to force core values from the top down, or from someone else onto you is a lot like plastic surgery. You can make the outside look pretty but if you don't fix the inside of the person, you haven't changed anything, really.

Or if you paint the outside of your house, but don't repair the rotted foundation or get rid of the abusive tenant, all you have is a pretty façade that is hiding the real issues, some of them dark and troubling.

This is not a new idea.

Lipstick on a Pig

To quote 18th century British physician Thomas Fuller, "a hog in armour is still a hog" (1732). Or 19th century Baptist preacher Charges Spurgeon, "a hog in a silk waistcoat is still a hog"

(1887). Or the 20th century variant offered by the Washington Post in 1985 quoting a San Francisco radio host who said, "that would be like putting lipstick on a pig" when describing plans to refurbish Candlestick Park instead of building a new stadium for the San Francisco Giants.

Bottom line, values work is something that cannot be faked.

Because it is so personal, this is something you have to do on your own. But don't panic. I have created a few tools to help you. You can use the tools in this book or download more in-depth worksheets by using the resources listed.

Find a quiet place to do this work. You don't want to be in the middle of creating your best life and have the phone ring or your boss pop into your cubicle with a routine question.

If possible, go outside and leave the routine behind. After all, Einstein says "a new type of thinking is essential if mankind is to survive and move toward higher levels."

New thinking requires new approaches.

In that vein, I have an important new approach for you – DO NOT RUSH! A lot of people are uncomfortable thinking about their innermost desires, or things that matter. I want to say this again. Do not rush this step. A lot of people are uncomfortable thinking about things that move their souls. That's okay. That's why this is incredibly personal work. You don't have to tell anyone about this. The most important thing is that you simply spend this time with yourself, and no one else.

You might find it easier to start by clearing your mind of the clutter that keeps you from focusing. If you are familiar with the practice of meditation, perhaps start with your go-to exercise to calm your mind. If you don't have any experience with meditation, you could try a quick, five-minute breathing exercise that I have found works wonders.

Start by sitting comfortably, with your feet planted firmly on the ground. Close your eyes. Focus on your breathing. By that I mean listen to your breath. Feel the air going in and going out. Do not force your breathing or begin taking deeper than normal breaths. Simply be conscious of the air moving in and out of your lungs. Feel the warmth of the air as it rests in your belly. Focus on nothing but your breath. Once you get into a state of focusing on your breath, count your breaths until you reach 30. After that, open your eyes. I think you will find that you have forgotten everything except why you came outside.

PS, this exercise also helps you calm down when things are getting stressful. Because it only takes five minutes, you can do it pretty much anywhere. Even on the toilet if you have nowhere else to find privacy. Been there, done that.

Now that you have quieted your mind a bit, look at the values words below. Contemplate them one at a time, saying each of them out loud softly.

Accomplishment	**Accountability**	**Authenticity**	**Adventure**
Authority	Balance	Beauty	Boldness
Compassion	Citizenship	Community	Courage
Creativity	Determination	Democracy	Fairness
Faith	Fun	Family	Grit
Growth	Friendships	Happiness	Honesty
Honor	Humor	Innovation	Justice
Leadership	Love	Loyalty	Openness
Peace	Prosperity	Respect	Service
Spirituality	Security	Status	Success
Teamwork	Wealth	Wisdom	Work-Life Balance

How does the word make you feel?

What images come to mind when you say the word.

Does any particular experience, or person come to mind?

How do you feel about that experience, that person? Are they feelings of love or joy or happiness?

Or feelings of anxiety, distrust, fear, or anger?

For example, when contemplating the word loyalty, what do you think of?

Do you think of a time when you were betrayed by someone that you felt should have been loyal?

Or do you think of a more generic image, such as a soldier in the Army.

In the first instance, you might find that loyalty is strong core value for you.

In the second, while you appreciate loyalty, it doesn't rank as high on your list as perhaps some of the other words.

Through this exercise, you're going to circle or write down the words that really speak to you.

You want to focus on the words that represent ideals you would give anything to have more of. Do you want more peace in your life? Do you long for a job that honors your creativity, or your innovation? How about courage?

Remember, there are no right or wrong values. Values ebb and flow over time, with some being more of a priority than others at any given time.

Allow yourself to be open to any value that speaks to you right now, in this moment.

Once you have identified six to eight important values, it is time to test them out. Write them down.

Consider putting these on pieces of paper you keep in front of you for the next step.

Index cards are perfect for this. If you don't have any index cards, you can make your own by downloading them from The Pink Briefcase. Links can be found in the final pages.

You can also download this as a worksheet from The Pink Briefcase. The worksheet contains about three times as many values words as the table in the book, but most people can find at least a few works that speak to them using the shorter list. Use whatever tool helps you feel complete before you move on to the next step.

Chapter 7

Step 2 – Dream Big Dreams (What Would You Do if You Knew You Could Not Fail)

"So many of our dreams at first seem impossible, and then seem improbable, and then, when we summon the will, they soon become inevitable"

~ Christopher Reeve ~

Keeping the six to eight values that you identified in the previous step, choose one area of your life that you would like to improve. This could be personal, professional, relational, financial, etc.

Note, this is not your goal.

This is setting an intention. For example, last fall I focused on improving my overall health. So, for the purposes of this example, the area of my intention is health. Any goals I set back then were related to health. Don't worry if you have lots of areas you want to work on. You can set as many intentions, and as many goals to help you fulfill those intentions as you need. We are simply starting with one.

Health is actually a value word on the worksheet. I will be honest; it is not a value word on my sheet, and it was not on my sheet last fall. But I have six other value words that do speak to me and for the purposes of Dreaming Big Dreams, we will walk through together how those values influence my decision to improve my health.

Your intention area may or may not be a value word, and even if it is, it may or may not be a value word that you've highlighted for now. And that's okay. You will see why in a minute.

After you have selected your area of intention, it is time to start dreaming.

What would do if you knew you could not fail?

What would your perfect life look like?

What would a perfect day look like?

What project would you undertake, what job would you have, what song would you sing, what book would you write, what person would you be in a relationship with, what animal would you own, what kind of car would you drive, where would you live, how much money would you have in the bank, how much money would you earn, what vacation would you take?

How would you spend your days?

Ask yourself these questions. Maybe ask yourself all these questions.

You can download these as a worksheet. Links can be found in the final pages.

Here you can see my answers related to my "health" intention.

What would you do if you could not fail? *Live to be 100*

What would your perfect life look like? *I would live close to my children and grandchildren and have the freedom to spend as much time with them as possible.*

What would a perfect day look like? *A day spent outside, in the garden, with my grandchildren playing with me would be heaven.*

Where would you live? *On a farm.*

What kind of job would you have? *I would like to make money from growing produce and flowers on my farm.*

What kind of project would you undertake? *I think creating a learning farm where people can take lessons on growing their own produce and canning, saving, cooking, would be fun.*

What kind of animal would you own? *Chickens, goats, maybe a horse.*

Some of those are crazy, right? I mean where did living on a farm come from? I have never lived more than 25 miles from the beach in my entire life. But right now, at this stage in my life, I DREAM of living on a farm and raising goats and growing vegetables and having chickens and smelling the smells of nature every morning when I wake up.

The point is, don't worry about how crazy these dreams might seem right now. We will go over that in the next steps.

Just allow yourself to dream the biggest dreams of your life.

The dreams that really get you excited.

The dreams that others might call pipe dreams.

The dreams that others might be jealous of you for having.

The dreams that make the hair on the back of your next stand up because they are so electrifying.

The dreams that when you think of them as possible, you are filled with absolute, unbridled joy and excitement.

But dreaming is only part of the process of goal setting. Remember all those New Year's resolutions? They started out as dreams.

I dreamed of running a marathon and we all know how that turned out.

What is it about your dreams makes you feel the way you do? Why do you want to live in a particular neighborhood? Why do you want a particular position at work? Why do you want to lose 50 pounds?

I will give you a hint. It's your values.

Take another look at your values. If you've written then on index cards, you can shuffle through them as you contemplate your answers to the questions.

For me, my quest to improve my health, and primarily deal with issues caused by being overweight, was because I value my family. Specifically, I have three grandchildren two and under that I love with my whole heart. I might even love them more than their parents, but shhhh...don't tell my kids.

A perfect day for me involves spending time with my grandkids and taking them to places I didn't have time to take my kids when they were young because I was too busy working.

I want to take them hiking.

I want to take them to the beach.

I want to ride bikes with them.

I want to be that cool Gramma that goes to concerts with their grandkids, bikes down Haleakala, ziplines across the jungle, climbs the ruins at Machu Pichu. And last fall, I couldn't do that.

Not because I couldn't afford it.

Not because I didn't have enough vacation hours.

Not because I didn't want to.

I couldn't zipline across a jungle because I was overweight. I couldn't climb Machu Pichu because I got winded going up the stairs to my office.

I value my family more than anything. I even value it more than chocolate. Yes, chocolate. And I did something about it.

Values in Action

Last fall I learned about whole food, plant-based eating. Yep. I've become a vegetarian. And not just any vegetarian. I am practically vegan. No meat, no dairy, no oil. Do you know how hard it is to find chocolate without milk or oil? Very. That is all I am going to say about that.

But this is working for me. I feel amazing. I look amazing if I do say so myself. I have lost 35 pounds without even trying. My blood pressure is down. My cholesterol is *almost* below 150 (153). I have so much energy I can run with the grandkids.

I set an intention (HEALTH), set some value-based goals (lose weight, lower my cholesterol, lower my blood pressure), and then focused on those goals. It took about six months, but it happened. It HAPPENED. I may not live to be 100. But at least it isn't my health that is going to stop me.

Let me be clear. This is not about being a vegetarian. It is about taking actions that are in alignment with your values. My entire transition to whole food, plant-based eating was easy because I had a picture in my mind's eye of the kids the entire time.

What are you dreaming of? And what do you value? How are they connected?

Ask yourself these three questions:

1. My big dream honors the values of ______________, ______________, and ______________.

2. My big dream honors those values in what ways?

3. The only thing stopping me from my big dream right now is ____________?

If you find it hard to answer these questions, particularly questions 1 & 2, then maybe you need to rethink the dream. You have to be able to tie your dream (goals) to your values.

Remember, I have been on diets before. You probably have too. But until I set a values-based goal, meaning I tied the goal to the value of living a long life with my grandchildren, I wasn't successful. I set the same Resolutions every December 31st.

So, make sure you can honesty answer these questions.

Are you still with me?

Great - On to Step 3

Chapter 8

Step 3 - Let Go of the Past

"I am not what happened to me, I am what I choose to become."

~ Carl Jung ~

Now, you have identified some values that resonate with you, and you have allowed yourself to dream the really big dreams.

That's all been rather fun, hasn't it?

Well here is where the work begins.

Here is where the rubber meets the road.

Here is where most of us let ourselves down and give up on our dreams.

Here is where the voices in our head tell us we are not good enough.

Here is where we allow what other people think dictate the future of our lives.

Here is where we let people that are too afraid to go after their own dreams put the chains of surrender on us and we stop believing we can do it.

We stop believing in ourselves. We stop believing in that spark of hope that lives inside all of us.

The only way to push past this is to let go of the past. Even if the past was five minutes ago when your significant other told you that you don't have time to start a business or your mother told you that you'll never lose those ten pounds (or 50) you've carried since high school, or your boss told you that you're not ready for the supervisor position you've been training for the past two years.

Let it go.

LET IT GO!

No one gets a vote here but you.

No one gets to tell you are not good enough.

You know you better than anyone. You know you were created for some great purpose. All of us were. You are not any different.

You have a purpose.

You have felt the call on your life from the moment you were old enough to think about the future.

You have heard the still, small voice in your soul.

It is the thing you dream about at night.

It is the thing you cannot stop thinking about when you have a bad day.

It is the thing that shows up on your list of Resolutions every single January 1st.

The question is, why aren't you doing something about it?

Stop listening to other people. Be respectful, but tell them no.

As my friend Brenda likes to remind people - You're not going to take it anymore!

Remember, we are all more than our worst mistake, or our worst day.

Do we stop loving our children because they make mistakes? Of course not. We never give up on the people we love.

Why?

Because we have hope that things are going to get better. We know from experience that things do not stay bad for ever. We have all had bad things happen that somehow, we manage to get through.

Well if that is true, then we have to let go of the negative things we are telling ourselves about our ability to achieve our dreams.

Earlier I mentioned that I volunteer with an organization that brings children to visit their incarcerated parents in prison. When I first started doing this, my friends asked me why on earth would I want to do that.

At the time, the answer was simple. It was not about the parents. It was about the children. Kids are most often the hidden victims of their parents' crimes. When their parents go to prison, they lose their relationship with them. They oftentimes lose their home. They lose financial security. They lose the only life they've ever know.

But by visiting their parents, they maintain a sense of normalcy. Studies have shown that kids who maintain regular visits with incarcerated parents perform better in school than kids who don't. Their incidence of juvenile delinquency is lower as well, ending the common cycle of family incarceration.

So, at first, I was doing it for the kids.

I went to prison. More than once.

But once I started going, I saw things I had never thought about.

I met one of the program organizers, a woman who served 19 years in prison for killing her abusive partner in self-defense. Her crime, and trial, was almost 30 years ago now. Had it happened today she wouldn't even have been arrested. But 30 years ago was a different time in the justice system. She was arrested, tried, and convicted of murder. And for 19 years the only contact she had with her son was through programs like the one she was now in charge of.

I saw an 18 year old son who didn't want anything to do with his incarcerated mother, and only came to escort his 11 year old sister, cry and crumple into her arms when she reached out to him and said "mijo" (my son).

I saw a heavily tattooed father holding his six-week-old infant for the first time, cry. Just like any other new father holding his child for the first time.

Now this guy was scary looking. He had more tattoos on his face and neck than I had ever seen. But he was crying. Real tears. Tears that only come from a place of pure, unadulterated love.

There was a person in there.

No matter what his crime, humanity still lived in him.

He was more than his worst mistake.

Now it is about more than just the kids.

It is about all of us.

We are all more than our worst mistake.

You don't have to be a convicted felon to spend time convicting yourself on a daily basis. It is time to get out of your head and into your heart.

We are all more than our worst day. Do not spend every day blaming yourself for what hasn't happened, or the things you have done to mess up your Big Dream. Let it go.

If you need to make some amends, then do that. But for the love of all that is precious and holy in this world, let it go.

Let go of the negative thoughts.

Let go of the things people say to you.

Let go of the things people say about you.

Let go of the feeling that you are not good enough.

Let go of the feeling that you do not have a right to be happy.

Let go of the feeling that what you have is all you deserve.

Let go of it all.

We are all more than our worst mistakes and our worst performance.

Let it go.

Chapter 9

Step 4 – Brainstorm Where you Want to Go and How You Think You Can Get There

"When it is obvious the goals cannot be reached, don't adjust the goals. Adjust the action steps."

~ Confucius ~

So where do you want to go? Of all those big dreams, of all those perfect days, perfect cars, perfect jobs, which one do you want to focus on first?

Let's say your big dream is to live in Hawaii. Having visited many times, I can understand why someone would want to do that.

For you, your goal would be "To Live in Hawaii". Yes, in case you haven't figured it out by now, your big dream *IS* your value-based goal. Because our big dreams come from that place in our spirit where our authenticity lives. Where the things that matter to us more than anything, our values, drive our thought process.

Goal: To Live in Hawaii

How do you get there? This next part depends on where a person is in their own life.

Are you of retirement age? It is a matter of simply selling your current home and moving there? Are you still working? If so, do you have a job that would allow you to transfer? Do you have a skill that is in demand anywhere, like teaching, nursing, computer programming?

Or do you really want to move to Hawaii and open a snorkeling shack on the beach?

Again, it goes back to your values.

What about your goal comes from your values?

Think back to the three questions at the end of Step 2. This dream honors which of your values? How does it honor those values? Understanding how your goal and your values are linked is critical to creating the right path to live the life you were meant to live.

For you Hawaii lovers, Do you value tranquility?

Or independence?

Do you value freedom, or do you value solitude?

The values will influence your road map. If you value freedom, you probably won't want to take your current job with you, unless you are currently a freelancer or other self-employed person. If you value solitude, you probably should look at Kauai or Maui over Oahu or the Big Island.

By filtering the goal through your values, you are creating a road map for success because you will be filling that hole in your spirit. You will be in alignment with that sense of purpose that was placed in you by the Creator of the Universe. You are honoring your values and living the life you were meant to live.

For me, my current values-based goal is to live on a farm. Why is this my big dream? Because I value my family and it falls within my intention area of improving my overall health. I want to grow my own food. I want to slow the pace of my life down. I want to share nature with my grandchildren.

Now you might be thinking "I love my family too and I want to improve my health, but I don't want to live on a freakin' farm!" And that's okay. The dreams that live inside me do not have to live inside you, and vice versa. They are my dreams. You have your dreams. There are no right or wrong values and no right or wrong dreams.

Last fall, when I spent some time working on my own values, I identified why I wanted to get healthy, and what I valued. Once I did that, the practice of getting healthy became second nature.

Diets fail because we don't tie the weight loss to a value.

For example, we say we want to lose weight because we want to look good. But why do we want to look good?

Do we want to look good because we value relevance and we grew up believing our overweight self was irrelevant?

Or do we want to look good because you want to start a new romantic relationship and think it might be easier if you were to "improve" your physical appearance?

The key point to identify is WHY you want to look good. It is critical that we know WHY we want to do anything.

Now that you have identified your goal, and connected it to your values, what do you need to do to get there? Do you need more education? Do you need to change jobs? Do you need to add someone to your life? Do you need to cut someone out of your life?

If your big dream is to have children, and your why is because you value family and nurturing someone else, it doesn't necessarily mean you have to start a new romantic relationship (if you aren't currently in one, that is). While some people might make their action steps around getting married or finding a life partner, others might create action steps that are around becoming a foster parent, or a single parent.

It goes back to WHY. Your values created your big dream, so it makes sense that your values direct your steps to get there, if you want to be successful.

Remember, you may have had some version of your big dream on your To Do list, or New Year's Resolutions for years, decades possibly. But we all know how those turned out.

Your big dreams failed because you weren't looking at your goals through the focused lens of your values.

Tie Your Dreams to Your Big Dreams and to Your Values and You Cannot Fail.

Make a list of all the things that you need to do to achieve your big dream. What needs to happen? After you list what needs to happen, list what you should do to make them happen.

For me, what needs to happen? I need to buy a farm.

Steps to get there? Identify where this farm is going to be. It needs to be close to my grown children because you already know how I feel about the grandbabies.

I also need to make sure I can afford it. I have to price them out.

If they are more expensive than my husband and I can afford then I need to adjust my steps. Do I earn more money? Do we look for a smaller piece of land? Do we move out of state?

This dream reinforces my commitment to stay healthy.

Here is the thing – I started this about five months ago, and I have lost 35 pounds. I've started a regular cardio exercise plan. I've started lifting weights. I AM healthier. I feel better. I am sleeping better. I have more energy. I am told I look better.

And I know that it is going to be a way of life for me now. Why? Because my values are driving my actions. Every time I look those babies in the eye, my heart sings. And I will do anything to keep making that happen.

Where are you going? How are you going to get there?

Are there people you need to consult?

Does your big dream involve someone else, like it does for me?

If so, are there any conflicts between that person's big dream and yours? Of course, it makes life a lot easier if the answer to that question is no, but what if the answer is yes?

What do you do?

You go back to your values.

Are there other dreams that also honor those values? Or are there baby steps that might be in alignment with your partner's values?

Instead of moving to Hawaii, maybe you start with a time-share there. That would force you to visit at least once a year, and trust me, you will see something new every time you go.

My point is there is always something that can be done that will honor your values and fulfill the big dreams in your heart. It just a matter of balancing the right value with the right big dream at the right time.

And no one can do that work but you.

Chapter 10

Step 5 – Put Your Big Girl (or Boy) Pants On

"It takes courage to grow up and become who you really are."

~ e.e. cummings ~

Now it's time to make it happen. You have got to be brave. You have got to be bold.

Although it takes courage, no one can make your dreams happen but you. And depending on where you are in your life right now, depending on what kinds of people you have close to you, it might get bloody.

President Theodore Roosevelt reminds us of this in one of his most meaningful post-presidential speeches from 1910, sometimes called "The Man in the Arena":

"It is not the critic who counts; not the man who points out how the strong man stumbles, or where the doer of deeds could have done them better. The credit belongs to the man who is actually in the arena, whose face is marred by dust and sweat and blood; who strives valiantly; who errs, who comes short again and again, because there is no effort without error and shortcoming; but who does actually strive to do the deeds; who knows great enthusiasms, the great devotions; who spends himself in a worthy cause; who at the best knows in the end the triumph of high achievement, and who at the worst, if he fails, at least fails while daring greatly, so that his place shall never be with those cold and timid souls who neither know victory nor defeat."

To achieve your big dreams, and live your best life, you have got to be the man (or woman) in the arena.

Stop talking about it.

Start doing it.

Don't let the criticism that you are bound to get affect your dreams.

Keep your values in front of you at all times.

Remember, you are not a tree.

You are not planted in the ground.

You can move.

You can move to Hawaii.

You can change jobs.

You can start a side business that funds your education so you can change careers.

You can write that book.

You can move to a farm.

Or a cattle ranch.

We live in an era of empowerment. If you are reading this book, you live in a freedom-filled country that allows you to call the shots in your own life.

It might mean having tough conversations with those we love. We might have to tell people we care about no.

It might mean giving up on an idea that you have been trying to force for 20 years and haven't succeeded in finishing. For example, another one of my big dreams was to be a published author.

Check mark!

But for decades I wrote fiction. I have to say, I was rather good at it. But I never got across the finish line.

Why? Because writing fiction was not in alignment with my values of mentorship, nurturing, and helping others succeed.

So, the dream was there, but the road map I laid out did not fit my values and consequently, I failed at every attempt. Once I figured out I could still achieve the big dream, and viewed the goal through my values, I was able to move forward and with this book, achieve the dream of becoming a published author.

You can do this. I believe in you.

This was a short chapter, wasn't it? Well, it is simple. Here is where the rubber meets the road. Here is where things can get simple, because you are focused, and determined, or get really ugly, because those around you are not willing to give up the old you.

The you that blew your Resolutions before President's Day.

The you that cares more about making other people happy than feeding your own soul.

The you that didn't understand it is not a zero-sum game. In other words, if you achieve your big dreams, it doesn't mean others have to give up theirs.

This is a big universe. There is room for everyone's dreams. Room for everyone's values. Room for everyone to live their best life.

You just have to be brave.

SECTION 3

Chapter 11

What's Next?

"The future starts today, not tomorrow."

~ Pope John Paul II. ~

Setting values-based goals is the link to goal achievement. Our years of failed goal attempts prove that. Mine included.

Now you have a new road map. You have a new perspective on the goal setting exercise. It is not just about the goal. It is about the WHY. Remember, there are no good or bad values. But you absolutely must know what values are driving you in order to set goals that you won't self-sabotage along the way.

What is your Why?

When we set goals that honor that Why, we set ourselves up for success.

Remember my marathon idea? Now, if I had framed that goal with the intent of improving my health and living to be a fit and spry 100, I might have stood a fighting chance.

But that's not where I was in my life at that point. I didn't have grandchildren. I wasn't worried about my health, per se. I was simply bored on my four to five-hour daily commute.

But today is a new day.

You can learn from your past mistakes and start planning the life you were meant to live!

You can set goals that honor your values and fulfill your life in such a way that it is indescribable!

You will feel more complete, more authentic, more alive than you have ever felt at any other time in your life.

I do need to be honest with you though.

It isn't always easy.

You know what you want. You have the courage to step up and step out. But still, it can be hard.

It can take time.

So, I have come up with some tools that can help you get there a little faster.

And if they don't help you get there faster, at least they make the journey a little more interesting.

Vision Boards

Vision boards are visual representations of the dreams one hopes to achieve. Without getting all "law of attraction" on you, people have been using vision boards since the beginning of time to envision the future they wish for themselves.

In their simplest form vision boards are pictures of the things you want to achieve. Maybe it is a car, or a particular house, or a particular job. Maybe it is a future partner or children.

When I was younger, first learning about some of the ideas in this book, I was a little embarrassed about the idea of a vision board. To hide that embarrassment, I made a vision book. I printed out pictures of the things I was hoping for and put them in a three-ring binder that I could flip through every day. I kept it on my bookshelf at work and carried it back and forth in my briefcase on the weekends.

The theory behind vision boards is that by keeping pictures of what you wanted in front of you, it helped you think about them. What you think about influences the types of actions you take. The types of actions you take influence your outcomes.

To that end, I 100% believe that vision boards "work". I will admit, though, with my vision book, my first attempt at a vision board, I was pretty superficial. It was 2010.

I put a picture of a particular wedding band I was eyeing, a picture of a motor home, a picture of a house with a built-in bookshelf that was phenomenal, and a picture of Cadillac.

I didn't really know what I was doing, but all those things were things that I wanted in my life.

When I would flip through the pages, I would think about ways to acquire them. While I was curious about the money part, I really didn't obsess about how much they cost. I just focused on having those things in my life.

What I found was that I would continue to think about them throughout the day. Not constantly, but a lot.

Do you want to know what happened? A few years later I remodeled my family room and built a bookcase. By that time I had completely stopped using that vision book. But the image of the bookshelf was in my subconscious.

The next year we celebrated a milestone wedding anniversary and I replaced my original wedding set with that band I had posted in my book. Two years ago I bought that Cadillac. Last year, we upgraded our tiny travel for a 38-foot monster that has room for nine. Nine!

Vision boards are not magic tools that help you get things you don't deserve or things that make no sense. But they do help you feel excited about your dreams. They also fill your subconscious with images of your dreams, and help form thoughts that can create ideas, which become plans, which become accomplishments.

To help jumpstart your values-based goal setting action steps, why not create a vision board, or a vision book, with images of you living the big dream. Keep those images in front of you when you start to waver.

Keep them close when people question your ability to achieve your dreams.

And remember, be open to all the possible ways those dreams can come true. When I put the house with the bookcase in my vision book, I thought it meant I would be moving. But the bookcase I built in my current home is every bit as beautiful as the one in the picture.

In other words, don't be so focused on the outcome that you miss the miracles that could be right in front of you.

Accountability Partners

Having someone along for the ride can be a huge help in achieving your big dream and living the life you were meant to live. Unfortunately, those closest to us might not be the most supportive. Don't take it personally. Many of them have seen you try things and give up. They have witnessed firsthand how you get depressed when you miss your mark. They have been along on this ride and to be honest, it wasn't always pretty.

But remember, this is a new day. You can do it.

I believe in you.

It is time to find others who believe in you too.

Social media is great in this area. There are Facebook groups for virtually every interest under the sun. A simple search for "Groups about Living in Hawaii" brought up over two dozen different groups. Looking for Goal Setting groups brought up almost fifty different groups. My point is everyone can find someone who is in the same boat as them and connect with them through social media.

If you don't want to work with strangers, why not look in your own network. You can talk to your co-workers about wanting an accountability partner without telling them the deep secrets of your big dream. Of course, it is better if you can be honest with your accountability partner about what your dreams are and the challenges you face in working toward your values-based goals, but it's not mandatory.

LinkedIn is another great resource for support groups. I am a member of several freelance writing and coaching groups on LinkedIn, and I enjoy helping people reach their values-based goals. The best part about social media and established networks is that for the most part, it is 100% free. If someone ever wants to charge you for joining their group, make sure you know exactly what you will be getting in return. If it doesn't come with completely guaranteed results, I would say thanks but no thanks.

Master Minds

One of the best books I have read about personal development is *The Law of Success* by Napoleon Hill. Written in 1925, Hill discusses sixteen strategies for achieving success in business and in life. He drew his inspiration from such business magnates as Andrew Carnegie, Thomas Edison, Henry Ford, and Charles W. Schwab, all of whom he interviewed at length. Followed up by his blockbuster hit, *Think and Grow Rich* in 1937, Hill is considered by many to be the "godfather" of self-help and business success.

Lesson 10 in his sixteen strategies is entitled "The Power of the Master Mind". The concept is simple. A group of six to ten individuals get together regularly to discuss their businesses, their goals, their problems, their challenges, etc., and collectively, the brain trust can solve just about any problem. According to Hill, Carnegie and Ford both used Master Minds throughout their business careers, as did John D. Rockefeller as he built his fortune through the creation of the Standard Oil Company.

Let's think about it this. You get four or five of your colleagues or other like-minded people together and you meet regularly, discussing what projects you're working on, what goals you are aiming toward, and offering ideas that the others might not have thought of. Depending on your big dream, a Master Mind might just be the tool you need to carry your values-based goal across the finish line.

Personally, I am a member of two different Master Minds, each with a different focus. One is informal and if you ask the other members, they might not even realize they are part of a Master Mind. We only meet twice a year, but those meetings are regular, and scheduled, and when we do get together, we have a defined program of reconnecting and offering help to the "tribe", as we call ourselves. The second Master Mind is definitely more formal, and we meet monthly to review each other's written work and provide input on works in progress. More than a writer's group, this Master Mind also provides input on the value of the work itself, as in, "are you sure this is the direction you want to take with this book" or similar ideas.

Master Minds might not work for everyone. But if you have a really complicated Big Dream, you might want to give it some thought.

And don't forget the most powerful tool of all....

Public Acknowledgement of the Dream

Remember when I said earlier that sometimes it is better to keep your dreams to yourself? Yeah, well, I wasn't entirely honest. But you weren't ready to hear this then. You are now.

Sometimes the most powerful tool you can have in your toolbox when it comes to setting values-based goals and achieving those Big Dreams is telling others about it. But you cannot just tell them. You cannot just say, like you have for maybe the last ten years, that you are going to lose weight, or go back to college, or move to Hawaii. You have put your Big Dream out there with conviction. You must own it. You have to have your values not only in the deep recesses of your heart, but in front of you too, all the time.

When those closest to you see you actually working toward your values-based goal, they will see you have changed. They will see that this time, you are serious. They might even help you get there. They certainly will be celebrating your successes because they can see how important the goal is to you this time around.

So, tell people if you want. Announce it on Facebook. Let your co-workers know. Share it at dinner parties. Talk to strangers on the train. Let them know about your Big Dreams. Say it with purpose. Say it with confidence. Act as if it has already happened.

You will be surprised at how many people start looking at you differently. In a good way.

Chapter 12

Are You Ready?

"The journey of a thousand miles begins with a single step."

~ Lao Tzu ~

You made it. You have learned the 5 Steps to Living the Life of Your Dreams. But it does not stop here. If it did, this book would be just another thing on your failed Resolutions list for next January.

Now is the time to act. Now is the time to put what you have learned into practice and start achieving your dreams.

Do it now. Before you let the voices in your head get to you. Before you forget the emotions you felt when you identified your Big Dream. Before you look at your in-box at the office and think there is no way you can find time to work on your Big Dream.

Do it now.

Spend some time with yourself.

Dream big dreams.

Let go of the past.

Brainstorm where you want to go and how you think you can get there.

Put your big girl (or boy) pants on.

Do it now.

Know that there will be challenges. Know that sometimes you will wake up and wonder if you have what it takes to make your dreams come true. Know that people, sometimes people you actually love, will laugh at you and try to talk you out of your dreams.

Stay strong.

Those people are, at their core, hurting. They are hurting because they feel the pain of missed opportunities every day. They see you excited for your dreams and think back to the time when they dreamt big dreams, mix it with a little longing about better times and what could have been, and they hurt. Their hearts hurt.

Stay strong.

Let those you love know that it is not too late for them to reach for their dreams.

Remember the man from prison? He has a lifetime ahead of him to love that new baby. Remember my friend, the program coordinator for the prison visitation program? She is the poster child for the idea that we are all more than our worst mistake. No longer bringing kids to prison, she now serves the "least among us" every day, helping them navigate the strange new world of freedom after incarceration. She is living her big dream every day.

As long as you are breathing it is not too late. As long as your loved ones are breathing, it is not too late for them, either.

So, go for it.

Be the poster child.

Be the one that lights the world on fire with their dreams.

Be the example your partner, or your children, or your co-workers, or your neighbors, or your grandbabies need when they talk about their own dreams.

I believe in you.

If you enjoyed this book, PLEASE share your thoughts in a review on Amazon. I consider all feedback a gift and I would love to hear from you!

Until we meet again....

Stephanie Dee Smith

Extra Resources

Values Words Index Cards –

http://thepinkbriefcase.com/vbgs/indexcards

Values Words Worksheet –

http://thepinkbriefcase.com/vbgs/goalsworksheet

Big Dreams Worksheet –

http://thepinkbriefcase.com/vbgs/bigdreamsworksheet

About the Author

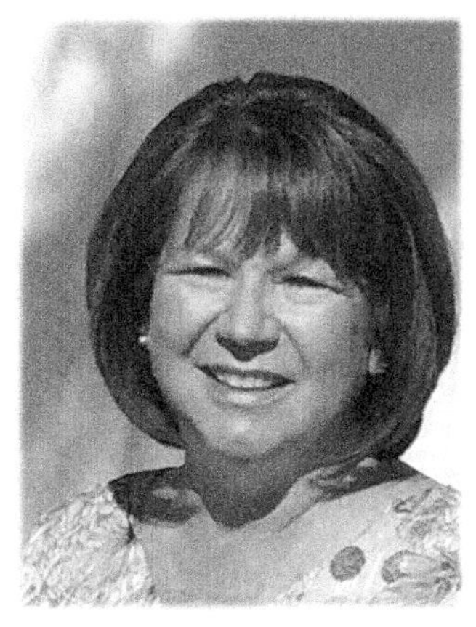

Stephanie Dee Smith loves to help people dream big and reach their goals. She has long believed that people can be anything they want to be and do not need to ask permission to follow their heart. Values-Based Goal Setting is the first of four planned books in her *Empowered Leaders Series* written to help people overcome the common obstacles that tend to derail them from achieving their goals and living the life of their dreams. Look for *The Creativity Habit* to be released soon.

She has spent most of her professional life in municipal government, having worked for four uniquely different cities in Southern California. Never one to believe that your job title defined your success, she moved from the clerical ranks to administrative to management over the course of 30 years and continues to inspire government leaders throughout the western United States as a workshop facilitator, motivational speaker, subject matter expert and trainer.

When she is not writing books or training future leaders, she enjoys crafting, gardening, camping in her 38-foot travel trailer with her husband, Jim, and playing with her grandchildren.

Made in the USA
Middletown, DE
16 September 2020

19948371R00066